ARMY

DELTA FORCE

BY NICK GORDON

BELLWETHER MEDIA · MINNEAPOLIS, MN

EPIC BOOKS are no ordinary books. They burst with intense action, high-speed heroics, and shadows of the unknown. Are you ready for an Epic adventure?

This edition first published in 2013 by Bellwether Media, Inc.

No part of this publication may be reproduced in whole or in part without written permission of the publisher.
For information regarding permission, write to Bellwether Media, Inc., Attention: Permissions Department,
5357 Penn Avenue South, Minneapolis, MN 55419.

Library of Congress Cataloging-in-Publication Data

Gordon, Nick.
  Army Delta Force / by Nick Gordon.
    p. cm. – (Epic books: U.S. Military)
  Includes bibliographical references and index.
  Summary: "Engaging images accompany information about Army Delta Force. The combination of high-interest subject
matter and light text is intended for students in grades 2 through 7"–Provided by publisher.
  Audience: Ages 6-12.
  ISBN 978-1-60014-822-4 (hbk. : alk. paper)
  1. United States. Army. Delta Force–History–Juvenile literature. I. Title.
  UA34.S64G668 2013
  356'.167–dc23   2012008552

Printed in the United States of America, North Mankato, MN.

TABLE OF CONTENTS

ARMY DELTA FORCE

Delta Force is a top secret group in the United States Army. Members of Delta Force call themselves The Unit.

ARMY DELTA FORCE

Founded:	**1977**
Headquarters:	**Fort Bragg, North Carolina**
Motto:	***De Oppresso Liber*** **(To Liberate the Oppressed)**
Size:	**Classified**
Major Engagements:	**Operation Urgent Fury, Operation Just Cause, Gulf War, Battle of Mogadishu, Afghanistan War, Iraq War, War on Terror**

Delta Force's main job is **covert operations**. The names and jobs of members are **classified**.

DELTA FORCE FACT

Members of Delta Force are called operators.

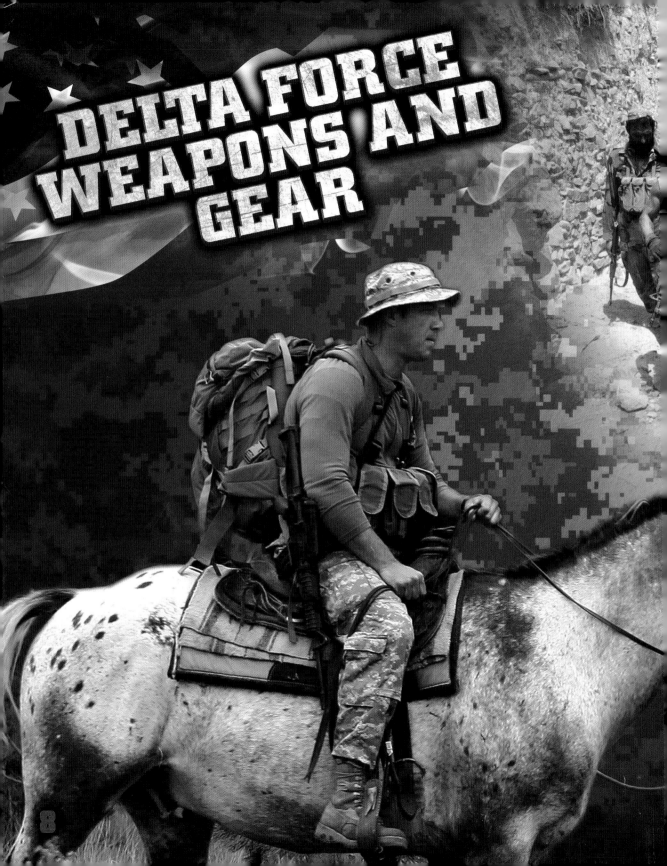

DELTA FORCE WEAPONS AND GEAR

Delta operators need to blend in with their surroundings. Most wear **civilian** clothing. They often use civilian vehicles.

Delta members use many guns. The HK416 **carbine** is one of the most common. Machine guns and **sniper rifles** are also used.

SNIPER RIFLE

HK416 CARBINE

Special gear helps Delta Force complete **missions**. Members use night-vision goggles to see in the dark. Global Positioning Systems (GPS) help them find targets.

GPS

NIGHT-VISION GOGGLES

DELTA FORCE MISSIONS

Delta Force performs **counterterrorism** missions. Members keep civilians safe.

DELTA FORCE FACT

The Army Night Stalkers often take Delta Force teams into enemy territory. The Night Stalkers are pilots who fly in the dark.

Delta Force also takes part in **direct action**. It attacks enemy bases and weapons. It may even carry out **assassinations**.

DELTA FORCE FACT

A Delta Force team has four or five members. Several teams form a troop.

Delta Force locates enemies and rescues **hostages**. Some members go undercover to gather information about **terrorists**.

Delta Force operators stay calm in dangerous situations. Their training and skills make them a key part of the U.S. Army.

GLOSSARY

assassinations—the killings of political or social leaders

carbine—a lightweight rifle with a short barrel

civilian—non-military

classified—declared to be top secret; classified information is not shared with the general public.

counterterrorism—military action that combats terrorists

covert operations—top secret missions; only Delta Force teams and the highest-ranking officials know of their missions.

direct action—immediate attacks on enemy bases and other targets

hostages—people who are captured and held in exchange for something

missions—military tasks

sniper rifles—very accurate long-range guns

terrorists—those who perform violent acts to create fear among people

TO LEARN MORE

At the Library

Alvarez, Carlos. *Army Delta Force*. Minneapolis, Minn.: Bellwether Media, 2010.

Besel, Jennifer M. *The Delta Force*. Mankato, Minn.: Capstone Press, 2011.

Riley, Gail Blasser. *Delta Force in Action*. New York, N.Y.: Bearport Pub., 2008.

On the Web

Learning more about Delta Force is as easy as 1, 2, 3.

1. Go to www.factsurfer.com.

2. Enter "Delta Force" into the search box.

3. Click the "Surf" button and you will see a list of related Web sites.

With factsurfer.com, finding more information is just a click away.

INDEX